Is Jesus in the Old Testament?

Basics of the Faith

Sean Michael Lucas, Series Editor

Is Jesus in the Old Testament?

Iain M. Duguid

P U B L I S H I N G

P.O. BOX 817 • PHILLIPSBURG • NEW JERSEY 08865-0817

Scripture quotations are from The Holy Bible, English Standard Version, copyright © 2001 by Crossway Bibles, a division of Good News Publishers. Used by permission. All rights reserved.

Cover photo: "Fiery Furnace" from *The Holy Bible containing the Old and New Testaments, according to the authorised version. With illustrations by Gustave Doré.* Courtesy of the Pitts Theology Library, Candler School of Theology, Emory University.

ISBN: 978-1-59638-634-1 (pbk)
ISBN: 978-1-59638-635-8 (ePub)
ISBN: 978-1-59638-636-5 (Mobi)

Page design by Tobias Design

Printed in the United States of America

◻ **Many Christians find** the Old Testament to be a difficult book. It seems full of obscure rituals, ancient customs, strange laws, and a mixture of inspiring and horrifying stories. It doesn't help that many pastors infrequently preach from the Old Testament, leaving ordinary Christians on their own to try to figure it out. Indeed, some churches have gone further than that. During a recent visit to the Mennonite museum in Shipshewana, Indiana, I was struck by the prominent announcement that Mennonites are "New Testament Christians," as if that were a separate category of believers.

Certainly many Christians live their lives functionally ignoring large parts of the Old Testament, either deliberately or because they simply are not sure what to do with them. Yet the apostle Paul was talking about the Old Testament when he said,

> All Scripture is breathed out by God and profitable for teaching, for reproof, for correction, and for training in righteousness, that the man of God may be competent, equipped for every good work. (2 Tim. 3:16–17)

The Old Testament is for Christians too.

What is more, this little booklet contends that Christ is present throughout the Old Testament. He is not merely present through a physical appearance here and there, or through the right interpretation of this or that Old Testament prophecy or type, but he is there on every page as the central theme and storyline of the entire book. Rightly interpreted, the whole Old Testament is about Jesus Christ. More specifically, the Old Testament focuses on and prepares for Christ's sufferings and the glories that will follow—that is, the gospel. As we shall see, this is the perspective that the New Testament itself teaches us to take toward the Old Testament.

However, I also want to explore what it means to rightly see Christ in the Old Testament. Not every attempt to discern the figure of Jesus in the Old Testament has been profitable. Some well-meaning interpreters have allowed their imaginations to run wild on this theme, so we need to learn how to read the story in a way that draws out what is truly there instead of inserting false connections to the gospel.

Finally, I want to look at some specific ways in which the Old Testament focuses on and prepares us to see and understand Christ and his ministry in the gospel.

WHAT IS THE CENTRAL MESSAGE OF THE OLD TESTAMENT?

Why should we expect to see Jesus in the Old Testament? The simple answer is that this is how the New Testament teaches us to read it. Recall the words of Jesus on the road to Emmaus. On that occasion Jesus caught up with two despondent disciples who were leaving Jerusalem after the crucifixion, unaware of the resurrection. As they walked in the gathering gloom of evening, he took them on a tour of the Old Testament Scriptures, exposing their woefully inadequate knowledge and understanding by saying,

> "O foolish ones, and slow of heart to believe all that the prophets have spoken! Was it not necessary that the Christ should suffer these things and enter into his glory?" And beginning with Moses and all the Prophets, he interpreted to them in all the Scriptures the things concerning himself. (Luke 24:25–27)

In other words, Jesus unfolded the Old Testament, showing them how it is fulfilled in him. According to Jesus, we should expect the message of "Moses and all the prophets" (that is, the whole of the Old Testament) to be Jesus Christ. Notice too that the disciples' response was not to be amazed at his cleverness in uncovering references to himself in such a wide range of sources. Rather, they were astonished at their own dullness in not having recognized before what these familiar books were about.

Nor was this simply Jesus' message on one particular occasion to those particular two disciples. In that case, the connection between Christ and the Old Testament might simply be an interesting footnote or sidelight to Jesus' main message. However, Luke 24:44–48 gives us the substance of Jesus' teaching to all the disciples in the forty-day period between his resurrection and ascension.

> "These are my words that I spoke to you while I was still with you, that everything written about me in the Law of Moses and the Prophets and the Psalms must be fulfilled." Then he opened their minds to understand the Scriptures, and said to them, "Thus it is written, that the Christ should suffer and on the third day rise from the dead, and that

repentance and forgiveness of sins should be proclaimed in his name to all nations, beginning from Jerusalem. You are witnesses of these things."

This is a summary of Jesus' master class in Old Testament interpretation, given during the climactic last days of his earthly teaching ministry. Notice the comprehensiveness of the language Jesus uses: "Everything written about me in the Law of Moses and the Prophets and the Psalms must be fulfilled." The Law of Moses, the Prophets, and the Psalms make up the three divisions of the Hebrew Old Testament, which Luke later designates "the Scriptures." In other words, the focus of his teaching was not on a few "messianic" texts here and there, but rather the entire Old Testament. According to Jesus, then, the whole of the Old Testament Scriptures constitutes a message about Christ.

Yet the Scriptures are not only generally a message about Jesus. More specifically, Jesus told his disciples that the central focus of the entire Old Testament is his sufferings, his resurrection, and the proclamation of the gospel to all nations, beginning in Jerusalem. The Old Testament is therefore a book whose every page is designed to unfold for us the gospel of Jesus Christ, accomplished by his sufferings and resurrection and applied through the outpouring of the Spirit on all nations.

Jesus' followers struggled to understand many aspects of his teaching during his earthly ministry. Yet this part of his message was clearly communicated to his disciples. Thus Peter says,

Concerning this salvation, the prophets who prophesied about the grace that was to be yours searched and inquired carefully, inquiring what person or time the

Spirit of Christ in them was indicating when he predicted the sufferings of Christ and the subsequent glories. (1 Peter 1:10–11)

Paul likewise declared to King Agrippa, "I stand here testifying both to small and great, saying nothing but what the prophets and Moses said would come to pass: that the Christ must suffer and that, by being the first to rise from the dead, he would proclaim light both to our people and to the Gentiles" (Acts 26:22–23).[1]

According to Jesus and the apostles, then, when you interpret the Old Testament correctly, you find that its focus is not primarily stories about moral improvement, calls for social action, or visions concerning end-time events. Rather, the central message of the Old Testament is Jesus: specifically the sufferings of Christ and the glories that follow—both the glorious resurrection of Christ and the glorious inheritance that he has won for all of his people. Certainly, understanding this gospel should lead to a new morality in the lives of believers. It should motivate and empower us to seek to meet the needs of the lost and broken world around us and should engage our passion for the new heavens and the new earth that will be realized when Christ returns. But the heart of the message of the Old Testament is a witness to Christ, which centers on his suffering and glory, his death and resurrection.

What Difference Does It Make?

This focus on the gospel as the center of the whole Bible, Old and New Testament alike, has several important implications.

First, it means that the gospel (the good news about Jesus' death and resurrection) is not merely the starting point of the Christian life from which we move on to studying ethics and learning how to be better people. Sometimes we act as if the gospel message might be necessary for those who don't know Jesus yet, while we who are believers instead need more guidance on how to live the Christian life. The Scriptures show us, however, that the gospel is the heartbeat of our lives as Christians, the central focus to which we must constantly return. The good news of Christ's death and resurrection is not merely the power by which dead sinners are raised to new life—it is also the power by which God's people are transformed into new creatures in him.

That is why Paul could say in 1 Corinthians 2:2, "I decided to know nothing among you except Jesus Christ and him crucified." Presumably, Paul was not saying that he preached only evangelistic sermons while ignoring the task of discipleship. Rather, he meant that every sermon he preached focused on the cross of Christ, the implications of which he then drew out for every area of life. To put it simply, he never preached Ephesians 4–6 (the ethical imperatives) without connecting them to Ephesians 1–3 (the gospel indicative). Our sanctification is rooted in and flows out of our justification.

Second, the chief problem that we face as believers is not that we don't know what we should do. In my experience, most Christians (including myself) know a great deal about how we ought to live. Our primary problem is that we don't live up to what we know. The gap is not in our knowledge but in our obedience. The eighteenth-century pastor John Newton once wrote a letter to a friend titled "On the Inefficacy of Knowledge."[2] In it, he lamented his inability to bring the profound doctrines that he loved so dearly to bear on the struggles with sin that he faced in his own life. I think we can all identify with his difficulty.

How do we address this gap between what we know and what we do? Sermons and Bible studies that focus on "law" (the demands of Scripture for our obedience), no matter how accurately biblical in content, tend simply to add to the burden of guilt felt by the average Christian. A friend of mine calls these sermons "another brick in the backpack"—you arrive at church knowing five ways in which you are falling short of God's standard for your life, and you leave knowing ten ways, doubly burdened.

In my experience such teaching yields little by way of life transformation, especially in terms of the joy and peace that are supposed to mark the Christian life. Focusing on the gospel, however, has the power to change our lives at a deep level. Through the gospel we come to see both the true depth of our sin (and therefore that our earlier feelings of guilt were actually far too shallow), while at the same time being reminded of the glorious good news that Jesus is our perfect substitute who removes our sin and guilt. He lived the life of obedience in our place and fulfilled the relentless clamor of the law's demands, and he took upon himself the awful punishment that our sin truly deserves. As the Holy Spirit enables us to grasp this gospel reality, he frees us from our guilt and refreshes us with a deep joy that motivates our hearts to love God anew. In this way, the gospel begins the slow transformative work of changing us from the inside out. This is what the nineteenth-century Scottish pastor Thomas Chalmers called "the expulsive power of a new affection": the fact that profound change in our behavior always comes through a change in what we love most, not through external coercion.[3]

This approach also suggests that the goal of reading our Bibles is not merely educational but fundamentally doxological—to move our hearts to praise and love our glorious and gracious God. Our aim in studying the Scriptures is not merely to know more ancient history or to learn useful life principles, but rather to be brought to see in a new way the glory of God in Jesus Christ and to bow our hearts before him in adoration and praise. As Newton observed, such study of God's Word will certainly change our lives as the Holy Spirit enables us to grow in our love for Christ and the gospel, but it will also enable us to glorify God even in the midst of our ongoing weakness and sin. As we read the Old Testament, therefore, our prayer should be that of the apostle Paul:

> Now to him who is able to do far more abundantly than all that we ask or think, according to the power at work within us, to him be glory in the church and in Christ Jesus throughout all generations, forever and ever. Amen. (Eph. 3:20–21)

HOW NOT TO READ THE OLD TESTAMENT

Some people have understandably been deterred from the kind of Christ-centered approach that I am describing here. They may have had bad experiences with people who saw Jesus behind every bush (burning or otherwise) in the Old Testament. Charles Spurgeon, for example, said that if he ever found a text without Christ in it he would go over hedge and ditch to find the road to Christ[4]—and if you read his sermons, it seems at times that that is exactly what he has done. Not every perceived connection to Christ in the Old Testament is valid.[5] So in this section, I want to look at various wrong ways to approach the Old Testament as preparation for learning to read it correctly.

It is helpful to begin with a diagram borrowed (and adapted slightly) from the late president of Westminster Theological Seminary, Dr. Edmund Clowney.[6]

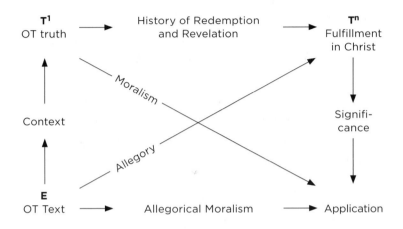

The first wrong way in which we read the Old Testament is what I have called the way of *allegorical moralism*, in which we extract a detail from its original context and apply it directly to our own lives without reference either to its original context in Scripture or to Christ and the gospel. For example, a woman visiting our church recently told me how meaningful Ezekiel 48 had been in her life. In the prophet's vision of Israel's future, the passage describes the borders of the different tribes, and she had taken away from this the message, "the boundaries of Dan need to be restored." This was significant for her because her husband's name was Dan and, as she read this text, she realized that her husband had not been keeping good boundaries between work and home.

While this observation may have been true and relevant for her life and could probably have been drawn legitimately from other passages of Scripture, this insight is hardly the purpose for which the Holy Spirit inspired Ezekiel to pen the chapter! She had moved directly from text to application to herself without understanding the flow of the text or the significance of its original context. A great deal of preaching in evangelical churches today resembles this process of interpretation: it is allegorical in that it fails to connect the passage with its original context, and it is also moralistic because instead of showing us Christ and the gospel, it simply seeks "timeless truths" or "life principles" in each passage to become guides for our behavior.

The next wrong approach to the Old Testament is *allegorical interpretation*, whereby people (especially preachers) fasten once more on superficial details of the text, but this time use them to find references to Christ where none was originally intended. This approach has been pursued with great popularity throughout the history of the church. For example, in a sermon on Ezekiel 40:6–8, the church father Gregory the Great identified the east gate of Ezekiel's temple as Jesus, the steps leading up to the gate as the merits of the virtues that lead to salvation, and the threshold of the gate as the ancestors of Jesus.[7]

In more recent times, a Christian author argued that the reason that the tent pegs of the tabernacle were partly in the ground and partly out of the ground was to teach us that the gospel is not just about the death of Jesus Christ (the part in the ground) but also about the resurrection (the part out of the ground).[8] While this doctrinal conclusion is important and true, I would suggest that the reason the tent pegs of the tabernacle were partly in the ground and partly out of the ground was simply that otherwise it would have been impossible to secure the ropes that held the tabernacle to them! We may admire the desire to connect the Old Testament to Christ, yet find the outworking of the methodology misguided.

In an effort to avoid the wild excesses of allegory, many modern interpreters have rightly placed the emphasis on understanding an Old Testament passage in the light of its original context. They encourage people to discern the message of the text within the broader concerns of the book in order to search out the intent of the original author in writing it. Having discerned this original idea, the next step is often seen as discerning the "timeless truth" that stands behind this particular historical writing.[9] What life principles does it teach us that are universal and unchanging? How can we then take those same universal principles and apply them skillfully to our own daily lives?

There is much that is right and laudable with this approach, yet I have labeled it *moralism* because of its inevitable tendency to place the reader in the center of the interpretive process and make the Old Testament fundamentally a story about us. In looking for universal principles of behavior that I can apply, this approach generally ends up urging me to "dare to be a Daniel" or "just say no to being a Jephthah." It flattens out the contours of the Old Testament history of redemption, and treats Old Testament characters such as Abraham and David as if their primary function were to model a life for me to live by.

This is the strength of Dr. Clowney's diagram, which reminds us that we must indeed begin by putting every passage of Scripture in its appropriate literary and historical context. We must start by seeing how this verse, passage, event, or institution relates to other verses, passages, and events around it. There is no place for the kind of allegorical speculation that takes a passage out of its original setting and completely ignores the human author's intent.

Yet we must also ask where this passage fits in the larger history of God's dealings with his people and what the divine

Author's intent was in including it in our Bible. How does this event or story advance God's program and point us to the great work that God is accomplishing in this world, which is the work of salvation in Christ through the gospel? How does this passage show us the sufferings of Christ and the glories that follow? For example, does it uncover the sins for which Christ had to come and die? How does it demand or demonstrate the righteous behavior that Jesus came to perform in our place? Only after we ask these kinds of primary gospel-focused questions can we properly get to the secondary question of personal application: how does this gospel then teach us to live in light of this specific portion of God's Word, out of gratitude for what God has done? Application is important, but the gospel comes first. What is more, even after we have applied a passage rightly to ourselves in this way, we constantly need to return once again to the comfort of the gospel's focus on Christ, for even as believers we will never live up to the standard of perfect holiness that God demands.

SEEING JESUS IN THE OLD TESTAMENT

The Incompleteness of the Old Testament

Of course, to talk about the gospel as the central message of the Old Testament is to assume that the Old Testament was never intended to exist by itself. Instead, it was designed from the outset to belong with the New Testament as part of a single book, the Bible. That is exactly what the book of Hebrews claims. The writer begins by saying, "Long ago, at many times and in many ways, God spoke to our fathers by the prophets, but in these last days he has spoken to us by his Son" (Heb. 1:1). He then goes on to assert that this

Son is superior even to Moses, the author of the Pentateuch and the supreme prophet of the Old Testament (Heb. 3:3–6). Christ's ministry is better than that of Moses, just as the new covenant is more excellent than the old one since it is enacted on better promises (Heb. 8:6). Quoting Jeremiah 31:31–34, the writer to the Hebrews says, "In speaking of a new covenant, he makes the first one obsolete. And what is becoming obsolete and growing old is ready to vanish away" (Heb. 8:13).

The writer to the Hebrews is saying that by itself the Old Testament is necessarily incomplete, even defective. God's purpose from creation onward was to have a people for himself who would live under his blessing. As Jeremiah pointed out, the problem with the first covenant was sin: God's people broke the covenant and were judged for their sin. This is true in the beginning, in the garden of Eden, and then throughout the history of the people of Israel, who repeatedly broke the covenant God had made with them at Mount Sinai. In the context of that history of sin, only a covenant based on God's free gift of grace to us in Christ could actually achieve God's purpose to make us his holy people.

Notice, however, that the writer to the Hebrews grounds his message about the obsoleteness of the Old Testament in the Old Testament itself! He quotes the Old Testament repeatedly to help his readers to understand the glorious greatness of the new covenant in Christ. In other words, to understand the climactic message of the New Testament properly, you first need to understand the preparatory message of the Old Testament. Only then will you be ready to understand the mission of the Christ whom God has sent. This is why many missionaries who translate the Bible into other languages do not start with the New Testament, but rather with Old Testament texts such as Genesis and Psalms. Without those foundational passages and their teaching about who God is and how he related to Abraham and his descendants, it is hard for people to grasp the message that this God has now taken flesh and dwelt among us in the person of Jesus Christ.

The Shape of the Old Testament

This incompleteness of the Old Testament is evident in its overall structure and shape. The order of the biblical books is different in Hebrew from that in our English Bible, yet both arrangements are made up of three distinct parts that point us onward to Christ.

The Hebrew arrangement divides the Old Testament books into the Law (or "Torah"), the Prophets, and the Writings. The Law is what we call the Pentateuch, the first five books of the Bible, covering Genesis through Deuteronomy. The second part in the Hebrew order is the Prophets, which includes the books of Joshua, Judges, Samuel, and Kings (the "former prophets"), as well as the books of Isaiah, Jeremiah, Micah, and so on (the "latter prophets"). The last category, the Writings, includes poetic books such as Psalms, Proverbs, and Job, as well as later history (Chronicles, Ezra–Nehemiah) and books that we would include among the prophets, such as Daniel and Lamentations.

This arrangement of the Old Testament highlights the prophetic dimension of the written history of Israel. The Bible is never merely a recording of the facts of Israel's story. Rather, it is the record of God's Word and its fulfillment, which is a prominent theme in Joshua through Kings. It also means that their Bible ended with the books of Chronicles, which serve as a grand recapitulation of the entire story of the Old Testament, tracing Israel's history from Adam to the return from the Babylonian exile and the struggle of the Israelites to reestablish themselves in their homeland. This recapitulation leaves open the questions, What happens now that we have returned from exile? Where do we go from here? As a result, the Hebrew order of the Old Testament has an "unfinished symphony" feel about it. If it is merely the story of a brave people surviving in a hostile environment, never quite being submerged by the stream of history but never quite fulfilling their potential either, then the reader is left thinking, *So what?* Is this the way their story ends, not with a bang but with a whimper? Are all God's rich promises to Abraham fulfilled in a small group of returned Jews, beset by problems within and without, clinging to a perilous existence in a small corner of their former empire? Surely there must be more to sacred history than this.

The same incompleteness is evident in the order of Old Testament books in our English translations. This arrangement was delivered to the English-speaking world by way of the Septuagint (the ancient Greek translation of the Old Testament). The Greeks arranged the books in their logical and historical order. They started with the historical books (which now also encompass the Pentateuch), slipped books like Ruth and Chronicles into their proper historical locations, followed the history with the poetic/wisdom books (Job, Psalms, Proverbs, Ecclesiastes, and Song of Solomon), and finished up with the prophetic books (Isaiah–Malachi).

This arrangement is obviously historically tidier, but it demonstrates a difference of perspective over the nature of some of the biblical books. For example, is the Pentateuch law or history? Is the book of Kings history or prophecy? Thinking about these questions shows the richness of the biblical materials. For example, if "law" means merely rules and regulations, the Pentateuch is clearly much more than that. It tells the story of the world from Adam's creation to

Israel's arrival on the brink of the Promised Land, and in that sense it is clearly intended to be history. Yet it is history that is told not just out of antiquarian interest, but for our instruction (which is, of course, included in the meaning of the Hebrew word for law, *torah*). Its central focus is the covenant that God made with his people at Mount Sinai, which is formative to Israel's subsequent experience as a nation, not merely a timeless set of rules to live by.

Likewise, the book of Kings may look a lot like the kind of history that one of Jane Austen's characters describes so vividly: "History, real solemn history, I cannot be interested in. . . . I read it a little as a duty; but it tells me nothing that does not either vex or weary me. The quarrels of popes and kings, with wars and pestilences in every page; the men all so good for nothing, and hardly any women at all—it is very tiresome."[10] The book of Kings certainly includes many quarrels of kings, wars, and pestilences, and it has its share of good-for-nothing men and even a few women, but it is far more than mere history. It is very interested in the fulfillment of specific prophetic sayings (for example, 1 Kings 2:27 records the fulfillment of the prophecy against Eli's family in 1 Samuel 3:12, and 1 Kings 16:34 records the precise fulfillment of Joshua 6:26). The writer of Kings belongs among the prophets as one who confronted the Lord's people with their failure to keep the covenant made at Mount Sinai and warned them of the consequences of their sin.

Even with this Greek arrangement, though, the Old Testament still ends up looking beyond itself. Now the final chapter is Malachi 4, one of the last of the prophetic texts, which concludes by anticipating the coming of the new Elijah:

> Behold, I will send you Elijah the prophet before the great and awesome day of the LORD comes. And he will turn

the hearts of fathers to their children and the hearts of children to their fathers, lest I come and strike the land with a decree of utter destruction. (Mal. 4:5–6)

Such an ending prepares the reader to look for the coming of a figure like the first Elijah, someone who dresses in a camel skin coat with a leather belt, who lives in the wilderness and calls down fire from heaven on people—in other words, someone like John the Baptist (Mark 1:1–8).

The three major divisions in the English ordering of the Old Testament correspond to three major ways of seeing God's hand at work in the world. The biblical historian reads Israel's history through the prism of God's revealed Word and demonstrates that God is sovereignly at work, whether on the front page or behind the scenes. The history of Israel is not a meaningless sequence of events, "a trash bag of random coincidences torn open in a wind," in Joseph Heller's phrase.[11] On the contrary, history is the story of God carrying out his grand plan in this world for the redemption of his people in Christ.

The prophet, on the other hand, receives his message directly from the mouth of the Lord and declares "Thus says the Lord" to his audience. He speaks of blessings and curses that come to God's people based on their faithfulness to the covenant. When Israel obeyed the terms of the covenant made at Sinai, she would be blessed. When she was unfaithful, she would experience the curses of the covenant. Yet that deserved state of curse, even when taken to its ultimate extent of exile from the Promised Land, could not be the end of the story. The Lord who had attached his name irrevocably to this people at Mount Sinai ultimately would himself do whatever was necessary to bring to fruition his covenant goal of having a holy people for himself (Ezek. 36:20–27).

Meanwhile the sage, the writer of wisdom literature, studies the world that God has made. He seeks to discern the order that God has created and to learn the wisdom of the Creator through it. Because the heavens declare the glory of God (Ps. 19), the sage can say, "Go to the ant" (Prov. 6:6) and derive a profound lesson from the simplest of creatures. He can discern the value of hard work, wise speech, and properly ordered relationships simply from observing the divinely ordained cause and effect in nature and human society. Yet none of this wisdom is ever merely secular and pragmatic. It always operates under the overarching slogan, "The fear of the LORD is the beginning of knowledge" (Prov. 1:7). In fact, the book of Proverbs not only begins with this assertion, it ends with the balancing conclusion, "A woman who fears the LORD is to be praised" (31:30). In other words, the fear of the Lord is the beginning and end of wisdom for all people, men and women, wise and simple, young and old alike.

Indeed, as the sage observes God's glory in Psalm 19, his attention is not merely caught by the rich diversity and profound beauty in nature. It is true that God's glory is visible in the colors of the flowers, the intricacy of the actions of ants and locusts, the majesty of the mountains, and the beauty of the skies. However, the psalmist's attention is focused on the heavens, and especially on the sun, which emerges each day like a bridegroom from his chamber, eager to run the course appointed for him (Ps. 19:5). In other words, what impresses the psalmist is the way in which nature joyfully and faithfully obeys the Lord's appointed purpose for it. This naturally leads him to consider the path that has been ordained for humanity to follow, which is the law of the Lord (Ps. 19:7–11). Why, when all the rest of creation is so happily obedient to its Lord, do humans alone think that they will find satisfaction and fulfillment in rebellion against their Creator?

Although these are not mutually exclusive or watertight categories, in broad strokes, there are three primary means of receiving God's revelation: through indirect special revelation (Israel's history), through direct special revelation (the prophetic word), and through general revelation (which is by definition indirect). These genre divisions themselves point us forward to Jesus, for he exemplifies all three facets.

To begin with, Jesus reads Israel's history authoritatively. For example, when his disciples were accused of breaking the Sabbath by picking ears of grain as they walked through a field, Jesus responded, "Have you not read what David did when he was hungry, and those who were with him?" (Matt. 12:3). He refers to an incident when David and his companions, because they were on a sacred mission from God, had legitimately eaten the bread from before the ark of the covenant even though they were not priests (1 Sam. 21). This incident becomes the justification for the actions of Jesus' disciples. After all, Jesus is greater than David, greater even than the temple: the Lord of the Sabbath himself (Matt. 12:6–8). In this way, the history of Israel in a profound sense exists to provide examples for understanding the work of Jesus.

As a prophet, Jesus authoritatively declares God's word to his people ("You have heard that it was said . . . but I say to you" [Matt. 5:27]). In Deuteronomy 18, God promised to send his people another prophet like Moses. This promise was partially fulfilled through a series of Old Testament prophets resembling Moses in important ways, yet it is only truly fulfilled in Christ. On the Mount of Transfiguration, Jesus shone with divine glory, just as Moses had on an earlier mountain, and the voice from heaven declared, "This is my beloved son, with whom I am well pleased; listen to him" (Matt. 17:5). The command, "Listen to him," is an exact repetition of Deuteronomy 18:15, where Moses said, "The LORD your God will raise up for you a prophet like me from among you, from your brothers—it is to him you shall listen." God himself was identifying Jesus as the ultimate prophet like Moses, the final mediator of the covenant.

Third, as the archetypal wise man, the embodiment of wisdom in human form, Jesus interpreted nature with authority as evidence of divine truth ("Consider the lilies of the field" [Matt. 6:28]). Jesus not only observed divinely ordained truth in nature, he lived his whole life on the basis of that wisdom. From his earliest days, his entire existence was dominated by the fear of the Lord (Luke 2:40). As Paul puts it, Jesus Christ is the wisdom of God (1 Cor. 1:24), the one in whom are hidden all the treasures of wisdom and knowledge (Col. 2:3). In other words, Jesus came to live the wise life on our behalf, not merely to show us what a life in harmony with our Creator's design looks like.

Jesus thus fulfills in himself all three divisions of the Old Testament: he is prophet, sage, and sacred historian, as well as prophet, priest, and king.

The Old Testament Story

Jesus also fulfills the storyline that runs through the Old Testament. It begins with the message of creation. The world did not happen by chance or through a cosmic conflict between the forces of good and evil. Rather, Genesis tells us that God created the universe out of nothing, as a place of order, beauty, and peace. Chaos is not the dominant reality in the world that God made, although from our post-fall perspective it may sometimes appear that way. God is the dominant reality in this world. At the very pinnacle of that perfect and ordered creation, God created the first man and woman to be in his image, made for relationship with him. God set Adam and Eve in a garden sanctuary in the midst of a beautiful universe, where he himself was present with them on a daily basis. It was truly paradise. All that Adam and Eve had to do was to keep that sacred space holy by obeying the minimal demands of God's law: "You may surely eat of every tree of the garden, but of the tree of the knowledge of good and evil you shall not eat, for in the day that you eat of it you shall surely die" (Gen. 2:16–17).

Instead, deceived by the serpent, the man and the woman chose to rebel and disobey God. That rebellion broke the conditions necessary for life-giving fellowship with God. They were thrown out of the garden, never to return. What is more, because all of us are covenantally related to Adam—he was acting on our behalf—all of us were implicated in his crime. As Paul puts it, "Sin came into the world through one man, and death through sin" (Rom. 5:12). One might have expected that the first sin would have been the end of the road for humanity, but at the very moment God convicted man, he also pronounced a word of hope. Sin shall not ultimately have dominion over us and win the final victory. God put enmity between the seed of the serpent and the seed of the woman and thus gave us life and hope (Gen. 3:15).

In the early history of mankind, however, it seemed as if sin and Satan might after all be victorious. Sin's seeds spread rapidly. In the days of Noah, only a few generations after Adam and Eve, the world was once again worthy of total destruction. Yet God in his grace kept a remnant alive, rescuing Noah and his family out of the near-total devastation of the flood. Even that object lesson of judgment had no long-term purifying effect on humanity, however. The brave new world that righteous Noah and his family built was only a few steps away from the arrogant godlessness that found expression at Babel (Gen. 11).

In the midst of the chaos that ensued at the end of Genesis 11, with humanity once again judged, cursed, and driven out, it might seem as though sin had comprehensively overthrown the order God had established in Genesis 1. Yet into that world of chaotic darkness, God once more spoke his creative Word in Genesis 12, separating Abraham from his pagan surroundings, giving him a new name and a new promise, and blessing him with a blessing that would be transmitted through him to all nations. In Abraham, God painstakingly restarted his creative work of making a people for himself.

Through many trials and tribulations, that people, Israel, began to take shape. In the time of Joseph, they went down to Egypt to survive a famine that was sweeping the ancient Near East (Gen. 37–50). Four hundred years later God brought them out of Egypt in the exodus under Moses. The Lord entered a covenant with them at Mount Sinai, in which they would receive the promised land of Canaan and be blessed in return for obedience to God's law (Ex. 19–24). Perhaps the high point of Israel's history was reached under King David, the king after God's own heart, and his son, King Solomon, who built the temple in Jerusalem. The geographic boundaries of the kingdom approached those promised by God. God established a new, everlasting covenant between himself and David's house and promised an eternal throne to David and his descendants (2 Sam. 7).

Yet God chose to allow his people to experience the worst of kings along with the best of kings. Indeed, even the best of human kings can swiftly become the worst of human kings, as David demonstrated by seducing Bathsheba and murdering her husband, Uriah (2 Sam. 11). Even good kings die eventually and are succeeded by people who don't match up to their standards. The end result of the depressing saga of Israel's history was, of course, the exile. The whole promise of salvation seemed once again in jeopardy. God's threat of exile from the Promised Land (made in Deut, 28:58–68) finally became a horrific reality. As the prophet Hosea put it, the chosen people had become "not my people" (Hos. 1:2–9). Was there any hope of a way back for the remnant of God's people after the exile? Humanly speaking, the answer would have to be no. Israel had broken the covenant too often and too comprehensively for any further forgiveness. Yet God does not see things as we do, nor does he measure things by our standards. He revealed himself to Moses as the Lord who is "merciful and gracious, slow to anger, and abounding in steadfast love and faithfulness, keeping steadfast love for thousands, forgiving iniquity and transgression and sin" (Ex. 34:6–7).

Even at the highest point of Israel's history, the dedication of the temple, the Lord looked forward and anticipated the lowest point, the exile, and provided a prayer for the people to pray in their hour of greatest humbling and need (1 Kings 8:46–50). If the people would simply repent and turn back to the Lord, the promise would be renewed in the midst of the judgment (Hos. 1:10–11). In place of the old, broken covenant, God himself would establish a new one (Jer. 31:31–34). Even the people's repentance would not be their own work; the Lord would replace their unrepentant stony hearts with responsive hearts of flesh (Ezek. 36:26).

How can such mercy and forgiveness be possible? How can the perfect judge of all the earth do what is right and still forgive transgressors? How can the Holy One of Israel take such persistent sinners to be his people? The Old Testament doesn't give you the answer to those questions. It affirms the fact that there are answers. All the pieces are in the Old Testament, like a jigsaw puzzle that has been freshly turned out of its box—there are prophets, priests, and kings, various sacrifices and offerings, a tabernacle and then a temple—but it takes the New Testament to put those pieces together in the coming of Jesus.

Jesus, the New Adam

Jesus comes first of all as the new Adam (Rom. 5:18–19; 1 Cor. 15:22). The Old Testament teaches us that we are all descended from Adam and Eve, who were not only our first parents, but also the first sinners. Genesis 1–11 demonstrated graphically how the children inherited and developed to the full that sinful nature from their parents. As a result, we are rebels against God not only through constant personal practice, but by our very nature. I remember teaching my children many things, from how to tie their shoelaces to how to read, but I don't remember teaching them how to sin. That came naturally to them, as it does to me.

We are all natural sinners, in the same way that some people are natural blonds. Some of us work hard at concealing our sinful nature, just as some work hard to hide their natural hair color, while others of us embrace our sin boldly. Either way, whether our rebellion against God is concealed or revealed, we are all born dead in our trespasses and sins, as Paul tells the Ephesians (Eph. 2:1). Just as a dark-haired person cannot grow blond hair, no matter how hard he or she tries, so a sinful person cannot possibly please God. Even the apparently good things that we do before we become Christians aren't really good because they come from sinful hearts. Our motivation for going to church, being nice, or keeping the rules is not to love and glorify God, but rather to make people think we are wonderful, or to suppress our guilt, or to achieve some other fundamentally self-glorifying goal. We cannot change our own hearts. We sin because we are sinners, and because we are sinners we stand under the condemnation of God. As Paul told the Romans, "All have sinned and fall short of the glory of God" (Rom. 3:23) and "The wages of sin is death" (6:23).

Since God is perfectly pure and holy, he cannot accept us just as we are. He cannot pretend that we are wonderful when we aren't. God does not lie. Indeed, how could we love a God who ignored sin or who pretended that evil was good? God cannot just ignore our sin any more than he could overlook Adam and Eve's sin. Our sin condemns us to eternal separation from him, just as it did for them. Yet God promised to send a seed of the woman to reverse our fundamental rebellion against him, putting enmity between Satan and us (Gen. 3:15).

God did that by sending Jesus Christ to be the second Adam. Jesus is the covenant head of a new humanity: just as everyone who is in Adam receives from him a sinful nature that leads to death, so all who are in Christ receive from him a righteousness that leads to life and resurrection from the dead (Rom. 5; 1 Cor. 15). That is why Luke traces Jesus' genealogy back to the first Adam. We were all once identified with Adam, inheriting his sinful nature and the punishment of death that came with it. But now, when anyone trusts in Christ, he is moved from Adam's kingdom to Christ's (Rom. 5:17). If anyone is in Christ, Paul says, he is a new creation. The old has gone and the new has come (2 Cor. 5:17).

Yet there was a terrible cost to our salvation, just as Genesis 3:15 warned: in order to crush Satan's power, the seed of the woman would himself be wounded. His wounding was necessary for our healing (Isa. 53). We have to be baptized into his death, so that by identifying with Jesus in his crucifixion—in which the death of the innocent in place of the guilty paid for our sins—we might also identify with him in his resurrection to new life (Rom. 6:3–4). Now the verdict of death is lifted for all those who are in Christ, and there is no condemnation for those who are part of his covenant people (Rom. 8:1). As our covenant head, he has tasted death in our place; the one has died in place of the many.

Jesus, the New Israel

Jesus is not merely the new Adam, however; he is also the true son of Abraham (Matt. 1:1) and therefore the true Israel. The genealogy in Matthew 1 flags that fact for you: it plots fourteen generations from Abraham to David, fourteen from David to the exile, and fourteen from the exile to Christ. Then, in the opening chapters of his gospel, Matthew shows Jesus personally reenacting Israel's story. In Matthew 2:13–15, like the young Israel, the young Jesus goes down into Egypt, brought there by a man named Joseph. Like the Israel of Moses' generation, Jesus survives the attempts of a hostile king to slaughter all the infant boys (2:16). In fact, Matthew explicitly cites Hosea 11 to illustrate the parallel: in Jesus, God is once again bringing his firstborn out of Egypt (Matt. 2:15).

After leaving Egypt, Israel next crossed the Red Sea, a deeply symbolic moment of salvation (for the Israelites) and judgment (for the Egyptians) involving passing through water. For Jesus, Matthew immediately focuses on his baptism, a symbol of salvation through figurative burial and resurrection in water (Rom. 6:4). John the Baptist was puzzled by Jesus' desire for baptism, since he thought of baptism as an act of repentance and confession of sin (Matt. 3:6). On those terms, John the Baptist needed to be baptized by Jesus instead. Yet

Jesus nonetheless submitted to baptism not for his own sins, but for ours. For him, baptism was an act of identification with us, a symbolic foreshadowing of the baptism of fire that was yet to come, when he would bear the judgment curse for all his people at the cross (Luke 12:50). This would be the means whereby Jesus would accomplish the exodus of his people (Luke 9:31).[12]

After the Israelites crossed the Red Sea, they spent the next forty years being tested in the wilderness. Likewise Jesus' baptism was followed by forty days and nights of testing in the wilderness. Even the form of Jesus' temptations echoed the wilderness temptations of the Israelites. They were starving and grumbled against God because there was no bread (Ex. 16:2–3). So too Satan said to Jesus, who was hungry from his fasting, "If you are the Son of God, command these stones to become loaves of bread" (Matt. 4:3). Instead of grumbling, Jesus replied, "Man does not live by bread alone, but man lives by every word that comes from the mouth of the Lord" (Deut. 8:3). Next the Israelites were thirsty and doubted that the Lord was really with them, putting the Lord to the test at Massah (Ex. 17:1–7). Satan next took Jesus up to the pinnacle of the temple and dared him to throw himself down, tempting Jesus to prove the Lord's presence with him by forcing God to deliver him. In response, Jesus said, "You shall not put the Lord your God to the test" (Deut. 6:16). In the wilderness, the Israelites made for themselves a golden calf and bowed down to it in worship, just as the Devil wanted Jesus to worship him in the third temptation. Yet Jesus replied, "Worship the Lord your God and him only shall you serve" (Matt. 4:10, quoting the substance of Deut. 6:13). Israel faced three tests in the wilderness and failed three times. Jesus faced the same three tests in the wilderness and passed all three with flying colors. Jesus was personally reenacting the history of Israel, only in reverse, succeeding where Israel had failed.

The crucial significance of this reenactment of Israel's history lies in the covenant that God had made with the Israelites at Sinai, which depended on their obedience for blessing. From the beginning, Israel constantly failed to keep God's law. This was no surprise to God; even in the days of Moses he had told the Israelites that they would fail to keep the law and would end up in exile (Deut. 30:1). The law was never given to the people of Israel to provide them with a means of attaining blessing through their righteousness. The goal (*telos*) of the law was always Jesus Christ (Rom. 10:4). As the new Israel, Jesus personally fulfilled the law for the sake of all who are in him. His perfect righteousness as one born under the law is now given to all who are his people by faith, so that our salvation might be through faith, not works (Rom. 10:9–10). Or, more precisely, our salvation comes not through *our* works, but rather through the works of another, credited to our account.

This is the significance of what theologians call the active obedience of Christ: as our covenant representative, he has obeyed the full scope of the demands of God's law given at Sinai, thereby meriting the promised covenant blessing of life forever in God's presence. Jesus Christ didn't simply come to earth to take away our sins. If that had been his purpose he could have proceeded immediately to the cross. Instead, he came to share our human experience to the full and to do so perfectly, completely without sin, so that he could replace our defiled garments with his own pure, clean garments of righteousness (as depicted in Zech. 3).

This incarnation of the people Israel in a faithful individual is anticipated in the Old Testament in Isaiah's servant of the Lord. Isaiah proclaimed that this servant would accomplish the things that were earlier attributed to the Messiah, bringing justice and light to the Gentiles (compare Isa. 42:1 with 11:2–4 and 49:6 with 9:2–6). But is this servant the nation of Israel, as seems to be the case in Isaiah 41:8–9 and 43:10? Or is he an individual distinct from the nation, as in Isaiah 49:5–6? The answer is that there is a crucial shift in the identity of the servant in Isaiah 49. Between chapters 40–48, the figure of the servant represents the nation of Israel. The people once rejected by the Lord because of their sins and sent into captivity in Babylon will be redeemed by the Lord and brought back to their land. Their hard service is over, and their sins have been paid for. Now they are called to bring justice to the nations (42:1–4). Yet the historical Israel that returned from exile was far from the ideal presented in this verse. The people were discouraged and disorganized, unequipped to answer the call.

In Isaiah 49, however, we meet a servant who both is himself Israel (v. 3) and yet at the same time has a mission to Israel (v. 5). Israel's failed ministry to bring light and justice to the nations is now taken up by the servant in her place. Unlike Israel, which was disobedient and suffered for her own sins, complaining that the Lord had abandoned her, this servant would be obedient, suffering in silence for Israel's sins, and looking forward in hope to his final vindication (Isa. 53). Who is this mysterious servant? Is the prophet speaking of himself or of someone else? The Ethiopian eunuch asked this very question of Philip in Acts 8, and Philip responded by telling him the good news about Jesus. Jesus is the personification of Israel, who takes on himself the suffering that Israel's sins deserve and fulfills Israel's neglected calling to be a light to the Gentiles, uniting in himself the two halves of the servant's mission described by Isaiah.

Jesus, the New David

Jesus is not only the new Adam and the new Israel, he is also the new David: "Great David's greater Son."[13] The Old Testament promised an eternal throne for David and his line in 2 Samuel 7. Yet David, the king after God's own heart (Acts 13:22), was himself guilty of adultery with Bathsheba and the arranged murder of her husband (2 Sam. 11). His son Solomon, the great architect of the temple, married many foreign princesses as the pathway to political security (1 Kings 11). Their descendants had an even more checkered history of faithfulness and unfaithfulness, until God declared of King Jehoiachin that even if he were a precious signet ring on the Lord's hand, he would tear him off and throw him away. Jehoiachin would end his days in exile, and none of his sons would reign after him (Jer. 22:24–30). The kings of Israel who were called to be Israel's shepherds had exploited and used the flock that was assigned to their care, instead of feeding and protecting it (Ezek. 34:2). It seemed as if the line of David was destined to come to a well-deserved end, in spite of God's promise.

Yet no sooner had God spoken those words of judgment over the reigning line than he added words of hope: the Lord himself would raise up a righteous Branch from David's line, who would bring justice and righteousness to the land (Jer. 23:5). In that way the Lord himself would shepherd his people (Jer. 23:4; Ezek. 34:11). This would fulfill the earlier prophecy of a new shoot branching out from the amputated stump of Jesse, David's father (Isa. 11:1). After the return from the exile, the Davidic descendant Zerubbabel was appointed governor of the Persian province of Judah, and his faithfulness in overseeing the rebuilding of the temple was a sign to the people of God's intent to recover the discarded signet ring and to restore the Davidic line to favor (Hag. 2:19–23). Israel's true king would come to her, riding on a donkey rather than on a warhorse, bringing salvation and peace to his troubled land (Zech. 9:9).

Jesus came to fulfill that expectation of a Davidic king from the moment of his birth in David's hometown of Bethlehem, itself orchestrated by the Lord moving the most powerful man in the world to decree an empire-wide census (Luke 2). At his triumphant entry into Jerusalem Jesus rode in on a donkey, visibly fulfilling Zechariah 9:9. In response, the children cried out, "Hosanna to the Son of David!" and Jesus accepted their adulation in spite of efforts by the chief priests to get him to disown it (Matt. 21:15–16). As king, he was responsible for overseeing worship in the temple in Jerusalem, so his first act when he arrived there was to clear out the moneychangers and merchants who were defiling it (Matt. 21:12–13).

Even though Jesus came as a king, he was not the kind of king the people of his day expected. They wanted a warlike ruler who would drive out the occupying Romans. Instead, he told Pilate, "My kingdom is not from the world" (John 18:36). Instead of fighting the Romans, Jesus healed the blind and the lame in the temple (Matt. 21:14). He transformed the status of those whose disabilities made them unclean and unable to enter the Jerusalem temple, as a sign of his greater work of transforming our status of spiritual uncleanness before a holy God by cleansing us from our sin.

Jesus accomplished this kingly mission at the cross. There, under what was supposed to be an ironic label, "the King of the Jews," Jesus looked nothing like the promised and anointed king (Matt. 27:37). Instead of being installed on a throne on

Mount Zion (Ps. 2:6), he was nailed to a tree on Mount Calvary, the ultimate sign in the Old Testament of a man who was under God's curse (Deut. 21:23). He resembled the cast-off and rejected line of Jehoiachin, rather than the beloved and chosen line of David, anointed and precious to God. Yet this is how our king redeemed and shepherded his people, triumphing over his enemies precisely through the weakness of the cross (Col. 2:14–15). His blood was the blood of the covenant that had to be shed to bring us peace and a future in the presence of a holy God (Zech. 9:11). The cost of turning us from prisoners of our own sins into the free children of God was his perfect life and death in our place, the righteous king standing in the place of his unrighteous followers, the good shepherd laying down his life in the place of his unfaithful flock. Only in this way could the king bring lasting peace to his rebellious subjects.

In the resurrection, of course, Jesus' kingship was fully vindicated. He was given the name above every name (Eph. 1:21), so that he is now the King of kings and Lord of lords (Rev. 19:16). He will return from heaven to claim the fullness of his kingdom, not riding on a peaceful donkey but on a white warhorse, armed for conquest (Rev. 19:11–15). The humble king who came not to be served but to serve and give his life as a ransom for his people (Mark 10:45) is now exalted to the highest place in glory, where he reigns forever on behalf of his redeemed people (Phil. 2:9–11). In him, the Lord's promise of an eternal throne for David's seed finds its ultimate fulfillment.

The Heart of the Old Testament

The ministry of Christ in his suffering and resurrection is thus the central focus of the whole Old Testament: he is the one toward whom the whole Old Testament is constantly moving, the one for whom as well as by whom it exists.

The Old Testament is not simply the record of what God was doing with a motley crew of religious misfits in a land in the Middle East, far less a catalogue of stories about a series of religiously inspiring heroes. It is the good news of the gospel that we have been called to declare to the nations, beginning in Jerusalem and continuing until the message has been heard to the ends of the earth (Acts 1:8).

At its height, the Old Testament gives us a glimpse in advance of who Jesus is. It gives us the categories of prophet, priest, and king that enable us to comprehend the ministry of the Messiah. In its many depths, the Old Testament shows us repeatedly why no one and nothing other than God himself in human form could possibly be the answer to our deepest need and provide us deliverance from our sins. The prophets, priests, and kings of the Old Testament all failed and fell short, just as we do. They all died without providing a ransom for our sins.

In both of these ways, the Old Testament prepares us for the coming of Christ himself, giving us the understanding of our fallen human condition that is the necessary prerequisite to understanding and appreciating the answer that God gave to our sin in Christ. Now, in these last days, God has sent his Son to accomplish our salvation: our Great High Priest has offered the once-for-all sacrifice of his own blood and has ascended into heaven to reign forever at the Father's side. As a result, we who once were far off because of our guilt and brokenness have been brought close in Christ, reconciled to God through him and restored to the Father's presence forever. Gentiles and Jews have been knitted together in the one new people of God, the church, and as a result, the Lord's name is praised to the ends of the earth (Ps. 22:27). This good news is the glorious theme of every page of the Scriptures, and it will be our song throughout all eternity.

FOR FURTHER READING

Clowney, Edmund. *Preaching Christ in All of Scripture*. Wheaton, IL: Crossway, 2003.

Goldsworthy, Graeme. *According to Plan: The Unfolding Revelation of God in the Bible*. Downer's Grove, IL: InterVarsity, 1991.

Williams, Michael. *How to Read the Bible Through the Jesus Lens: A Guide to Christ-Focused Reading of Scripture*. Grand Rapids: Zondervan, 2012.

CHRIST-CENTERED EXPOSITIONS OF THE OLD TESTAMENT

Johnson, Dennis E., ed. *Heralds of the King: Christ-centered Sermons in the Tradition of Edmund P. Clowney*. Wheaton, IL: Crossway, 2009.

The Gospel According to the Old Testament series, published by P&R.

The Reformed Expository Commentary series, published by P&R.

NOTES

1. These are just two of many similar New Testament passages (e.g., Acts 3:18, 21, 24; 17:2–3). For a fuller exploration, see Edmund P. Clowney, "Preaching Christ from All the Scriptures," in S. T. Logan (ed.), *The Preacher and Preaching* (Phillipsburg, NJ: Presbyterian and Reformed, 1986), 164; see also Bryan Chapell, *Christ-Centered Preaching. Redeeming the Expository Sermon* (Grand Rapids: Baker, 1996), 272.

2. John Newton, "On the Inefficacy of Knowledge" in *The Works of John Newton* (Carlisle, PA: Banner of Truth, 1985 reprint), 1.245–53.

3. Thomas Chalmers, "The Expulsive Power of a New Affection" in *Sermons and Discourses* (New York: Robert Carter & Brothers, 1877), 2.271–77.

4. Charles Spurgeon, "How to Read the Bible," a sermon preached in 1879 at the Metropolitan Tabernacle in London, http://www.spurgeon .org/sermons/1503.htm (accessed June 8, 2012).

5. Spurgeon himself warns of making connections that strain credulity—for example, the preacher who spoke about the Trinity from the three baskets on the head of Pharaoh's baker (*Lectures to My Students* [Grand Rapids: Zondervan, 1972 reprint], 97).

6. Adapted from Edmund Clowney, *Preaching Christ in All of Scripture* (Wheaton, IL: Crossway, 2003), 32.

7. *The Homilies of Gregory the Great on the Book of the Prophet Ezekiel*, trans. T. Gray (Etna, CA: Center for Traditionalist Orthodox Studies, 1990), 179–85.

8. Martin R. DeHaan, *The Tabernacle* (Grand Rapids: Zondervan, 1955), 37, 65.

9. See, for example, Steven Mathewson, *The Art of Preaching Old Testament Narrative* (Grand Rapids: Baker, 2002), 101. Mathewson certainly wants to avoid moralism (see pp. 102–103), yet his method of application inevitably pushes him in that direction.

10. *Northanger Abbey* (London: Penguin, 2003), 104.

11. Joseph Heller, *Good as Gold* (New York: Simon & Schuster, 1979).

12. The word which the ESV translates as "departure" in this verse is literally in the Greek the "exodus," which Jesus was about to accomplish in Jerusalem.

13. James Montgomery, "Hail to the Lord's Anointed," 1821.

CHRIST-CENTERED STUDIES OF THE OLD TESTAMENT FROM P&R

"A tremendous resource." —Tim Keller

Written for laypeople and pastors, The Gospel According to the Old Testament series examines the lives of Old Testament characters. It is designed to encourage Christ-centered reading, teaching, and preaching of the Old Testament.

ALSO IN THE SERIES:

After God's Own Heart, Mark J. Boda
Crying Out for Vindication, David R. Jackson
Faith in the Face of Apostasy, Raymond B. Dillard
From Famine to Fullness, Dean R. Ulrich
Hope in the Midst of a Hostile World, George M. Schwab
Immanuel in Our Place, Tremper Longman III
Living in the Gap Between Promise and Reality, Iain M. Duguid
Living in the Light of Inextinguishable Hope, Iain M. Duguid
Longing for God in an Age of Discouragement, Bryan R. Gregory
Love Divine and Unfailing, Michael P. V. Barrett
Salvation Through Judgment and Mercy, Bryan D. Estelle